A
HANDBOOK
FOR THOSE
WORKING WITH
THE ELDERLY

LOOKING AT
CONFUSION

D0543945

WINSLOW PRESS

Telford Road, Bicester, Oxon OX6 0TS Tel : Bicester (0869) 244644

First published in 1987 by
Winslow Press Ltd, Telford Road, Bicester, Oxon OX6 0TS
Reprinted 1988, 1989, 1990, 1992, 1994

ISBN 0 86388 060 6

WP285/Printed in Great Britain by Hobbs the Printers of Southampton

Contents

This book is dedicated to the post-graduate trainees in clinical psychology, and participants of various courses whose enquiring minds forced me to consider what I meant by the word 'dementia'.

Preface

This book is the result of a growing awareness of the confusion that exists among staff, at all levels, about the meaning and implications of the word 'dementia'. It has become obvious that there is a need to improve knowledge and understanding of this aspect of the ageing process. Even when presented with the facts, the audience—students or otherwise—finds it hard to accept them. Those with years of experience in the caring role are often stunned to hear that dementia is not a disease in its own right, and that some forms are reversible. Many training schemes appear to have skimmed over this issue. There is a reluctance amongst professionals to define their terms clearly, or to provide a working definition which will aid staff in the provision of a relevant and effective service for their clients.

The aims of this book, therefore, are:

1 to present a logical way of looking at and understanding the many facets of dementia;

2 to help in establishing a useful working concept of dementia;

3 to assist an individual interested in the problems of the elderly to think carefully about illness and dementing processes;

4 to provide some ideas for training programmes on the subject;

5 to provoke an increase in understanding and information which will be of benefit to the elderly.

Discussion topics and exercises are listed, usually at the beginning of a chapter. These are intended to provoke thought, to help the individual to become conscious of his or her own attitudes or beliefs and to increase awareness of the issues to be considered.

The subject is contentious, controversial and provocative. If these few chapters do nothing else but incite arguments about their attempt at logic, they will have achieved their purpose.

Una Holden-Cosgrove
June 1987

1

Confusion

Discussion Topics

■What does the word 'confusion' mean to you? Try to define it.

■Does everyone in the group agree, or are there strong differences of opinion?

A dictionary definition states: '*Confusion*—a state of disorder, perplexity, or bewilderment'. A medical handbook would list the main features of acute confusion as follows:

Disorientation—patients who do not know who they are, where they are, who other people are and may lack knowledge of time and place.

Withdrawal can occur.

Behaviour becomes strange—a person can talk nonsense, become hostile or apathetic, perform tasks incorrectly and have 'funny' ideas.

Feelings of distress are common—agitation, anxiety and mood changes can occur.

Self-care may be neglected, day and night may be mixed up.

Although the signs outlined are typical, in practice this 'state of disorder' may occur for many reasons. Confusion about confusion is rife, not only among lay people; even hospital and social services staff are unsure and will use the term to cover a variety of responses and situations.

To clarify the picture it is useful to consider the general use of the word.

Exercise

Encourage a group to discuss actual occurrences of confusion and to consider what might have been the cause. Use a board or flip chart to record responses with numbers as indicated below. Do not explain the significance of the numbers until suggestions have ceased.

Numbers can be used to indicate the following possibilities:

1 A probable real deterioration process is present. Organic disorders.

2 Delirium due to physical illness.

3 Neurological problems.

4 Psychiatric disturbances.

5 Daily living events.

6 Daily living excesses.

7 Environmental influences.

8 Changes in normal living—shock, bereavement, anaesthetics, stress etc.

Confusion can affect anyone, of any age, and for a variety of reasons in a variety of circumstances. If the group has not included more general examples of confusion, point out the fact that all of us can suffer from confusion at some moment in our lives. 'When were *you* last confused?' usually opens up new avenues of thought.

Any of the following could be termed 'confusion' (the appropriate category number is in brackets after each situation).

'I know I put the spice on that shelf' (5).

'I didn't mean Chagford, I meant Chagley' (5 or 1).

'I forgot to turn the gas off' (1, 4, 5 or 8).

(Referring to old school friends) 'After all those years I don't know which is Jean and which is Mary' (5).

Pouring milk into a teapot (1, 2, 5 or 6).

The after-effects of a drinking session (6).

Finding the way around a strange town, waking up in a strange bed (7).

Driving in another country, using a foreign language without recent practice (5 or 8).

Not recognising familiar people (1, 2, 3, 4 or 6).

Sleep-walking and waking up (3, 5 or 6).

Anaesthetics and recovery (8).

Drugs—either self-inflicted or medical (6 or 8).

Regaining consciousness after a head injury, coma, severe illness (3, 2 or 8).

Confusion can be either a temporary or prolonged state, during which a person acts in a mixed-up manner, or feels mixed-up. Even a child can be confused in a day to day situation—tying shoe laces or writing from right to left instead of left to right. The more simple forms of confusion are tolerated, treated with sympathy or even amusement, as such states are transient. The more profound forms are seen in a more serious light. If the confusion persists it can prove frightening and provoke anxiety in the person and their relatives or friends to such an extent that erroneous conclusions are reached.

Stress at work or home can lead to a more persistent form of confusion, which, though not organic in nature, has serious emotional consequences. Under pressure, work suffers, mistakes are made and a job might be lost. Under personal stress, daily living skills can be disturbed too. Objects are dropped, food is burned, ingredients omitted and housework or home tasks neglected—even personal appearance can suffer.

Physical illness can lead to a person becoming confused, which means that diagnosis can become difficult. A treatable illness can be overlooked with the elderly who show signs of disorientation and poor self-care. Expectations about the presence of a deterioration process are more likely when the perplexed person is over the age of 65. The confusion may well be due to something other than a deterioration process and should be fully investigated before unfounded conclusions are reached.

Further Exercises

- When you were confused what were the reactions of others?
- List some situations where people could become confused.
- List the sorts of behaviours or responses associated with confusion.
- List examples of childhood confusions.
- List day-to-day examples of confusion that could cause embarrassment.
- What physical disabilities could cause confusion? In what way?
- What are the common reactions to confusion and age?
- What role could drugs, glue-sniffing, etc. play in confusing people?

USEFUL DEFINITIONS

A few of the terms used throughout this book may be unfamiliar; some of them are outlined below.

Apraxia An inability to perform voluntary actions which is not due to disability of muscle, limb or understanding. The movement or action can be performed automatically, or when the person is not thinking about it.

Aphasia Language disorders which include difficulties with speech, reading, writing, calculation etc.

Agnosia Impairments in recognition of sensory input—what is seen, heard, touched or tasted. The difficulty is not due to a deficit in the sensory system concerned, to intelligence or to unfamiliarity with the object, sound etc.

Agraphia Disorders of writing.

Acalculia Disorders of calculation.

Ataxia Disorders of gait, staggering or unusual ways of walking.

Anosognosia A body image disorder where the patient neglects or ignores the diseased part of his or her body. Denial of damage or even denial of ownership of that part of the body can occur.

Alzheimer's Disease *see Chapter 10.* The most frequent cause of intellectual and social deterioriation.

Hydrocephalus In general this refers to an enlargement of the cerebral ventricles of the brain. There are different types.

Korsakow's Psychosis This, and **Wernicke's Syndrome** are associated with deficiencies of the vitamin thiamine in some chronic alcoholics. A dilapidated mental state is a common factor with amnesia being a notable feature.

Wilson's Disease Associated with abnormal copper metabolism causing changes in mental functioning.

Encephalitis A generalised infection of the brain usually caused by a viral invasion.

Neurons The basic cell units of the nervous system which are responsible for the conduction of impulses and are important in many vital functions.

Dendrites Little projections from the cell body which pick up impulses from other neurons and send them *back* into the cell body. The axon is the projection which conducts impulses *out* to other neurons.

Neurotransmitters The chemical mediators which facilitate the passage of impulses from axon to dendrite.

2

Delirium

Discussion Topics

■ Define Delirium. When does it occur?

■ What would you do if a small child was staggering about, talking rubbish, appeared flushed and kept falling asleep or crying?

■ What would you think if a person over 65-years-old showed similar behaviour?

The dictionary defines delirium as a wandering in the mind, lightheadedness, or a mental disturbance caused by grave, physical illness or nervous shock. This is quite reasonable as the medical diagnostic signs are:

A clouded state of consciousness.

An acute onset.

The patient is awake and can respond, but may be dozy and unable to make sensible responses.

Attention is impaired. Thinking is disordered.

Short-term memory is poor and there is poor recognition of sensory input—inability to recognise what is seen, heard, etc.

There are fluctuations in mood, night-time disturbances are common.

There are impairments in the processing of external and internal information—in other words the patient is unclear where pain is located and cannot understand what is happening around him/her.

They are disorientated in time, place and person. They do not know where they are, who people are, nor the date, day or time.

There is a disturbance in sleeping and wakefulness.

Hallucinations and delusions may be present—a chair may become a tiger, the nurse an attacker, etc.

Delirium is yet another form of confusion, but one of a serious nature. Medical aid is indicated so that thorough investigations can be carried out and appropriate treatment measures provided.

Delirium is something everyone understands, something that most people have either experienced for themselves or observed with other people. Temperatures are commonplace, poisons and fevers can cause temporary disturbances during which a person can do or say silly things—such situations and reactions are generally known about. On recovery from a delirious state the patient will frequently ask 'Did I do or say anything awful?' They may laugh at their unremembered behaviour, but usually they refuse to believe that they could have been so outrageous.

Delirium tremens is well recognised as a reaction associated with massive consumption of alcohol. Delusions and hallucinations in this state are common. All the 'pink elephants', mythical creatures and strange experiences reported by individuals are often associated with alcoholic excess rather than a psychosis.

The causes of delirium could make a very lengthy list; the following possible causes are only a sample of the illnesses to which a delirium is related:

Anaemia	Viruses, influenza etc.
Carcinoma	Renal failure
Cardiac failure	Drug intoxication
Respiratory failure	Endocrine disturbance
Hypothermia	Electrolyte disturbance

The viruses include many varieties of influenza. Most childhood complaints—measles, chicken-pox etc—can also produce a delirium. Children can run a high temperature overnight and be out to play the next day. Prisoners of war on an inappropriate diet, and possibly also subjected to intense climatic conditions, may frequently become confused and delirious. Survivors from such conditions may still suffer from the after-effects and treatment with selected vitamins may be necessary throughout life in order to combat them.

Severe shock can have a similar effect to physical illness. People who have been involved in a road accident or faced with a sudden bereavement or other traumatic event may become delirious. Age has nothing to do with delirium. It can occur at any age. A person aged more than 60 who shows signs of confusion or delirium is probably more likely to be suffering from a physical disorder than from a state related to mental deterioration. Without a thorough and relevant investigation there is no way of knowing the cause, or of obtaining a true picture. A person aged over 60 has as much right to such an investigation as a person of any other age. Investigation methods have improved considerably over the years and the idea that laboratory or other aids to diagnosis could prove dangerous for the elderly is no longer held to be the case. With a proper diagnosis, appropriate treatment can be offered and the physical illness will be cured or minimised just as it would be for any other age group.

Discussion Topics

■ Describe a personal experience of a delirium.

■ Think of situations you have encountered when an elderly person became delirious.

■ Have you encountered a situation when a person was thought to be deteriorating mentally but was later found to have a physical disorder?

■ List the differences between daily living types of confusion and a delirium.

■ Examine the changes in technology and laboratory investigations which make it less hazardous to investigate illness in the elderly today.

■ Discuss in small groups the part that expectations play in missing a correct diagnosis of an illness, or in mixing up such an illness with a deterioration process. Discuss your ideas with other groups.

3
Depression

Discussion Topics

■ Have you been ill during the last few months? Or for a long time at any point in your life?

■ How did you feel when you were beginning to recover, particularly when you were on your own for a number of hours or days?

■ Have you ever been close to someone suffering from a bereavement?

■ How would *you* survive if imprisoned in solitary confinement for weeks or months?

Isolation or emotional upheaval, for whatever reason, has a profound effect on our self-esteem, confidence and inner strength. When we have been ill for some time, or prevented from pursuing our normal activities, living patterns and social outlets, we become weakened. We become resentful of the limits imposed on our independence, angered by enforced dependence on others and begin to feel that the situation will never end. Or that even when or if it does, we have lost our capabilities and may well be unable to function normally ever again.

Of course, different people react in different ways to adversity. Many remarkable stories are told about incredible people who survive very long periods of incarceration and isolation as political or wartime prisoners, and just as many are told about people who survive devastating illnesses. However, the average person is in dread of total isolation, social deprivation or limiting physical disorders. The most severe form of torture is sensory and social deprivation, as this can prove so damaging intellectually and emotionally.

A considerable number of elderly people *are* socially isolated, live alone, rarely go out and have no family or friends to visit them. Their home becomes their prison, even though it remains precious to them, but they are stressed by the deprivation that results. Under such duress depression flourishes.

The dictionary defines depression as a despondency, dejection or diminished vigour. This throws no light on the degree, the duration or the cause. Psychiatric and medical literature generally provide greater detail and those wishing for a full account should consult the relevant books and articles. Here, the concern is to relate depression to the mythology of dementia and to emphasise its frequency and the need to consider that observed behaviour might be due to an emotional state rather than to an organic one.

First of all, how can someone tell if a person is depressed? It is not an easy matter to differentiate the pattern of a dementia process from that of a depression, so misdiagnosis can occur.

The main features of a depression are:

There is a sadness about the person. Guilt, self-reproach or helplessness may be expressed.

Delusions about bodily change may be present.

There is, apparently, a disturbance in intellectual function.

Symptoms may imitate hypochondriasis.

Panic reactions may occur.

Physical appearance, in the presence of apathy, may have deteriorated.

Early waking and poor appetite; other normal functions are disturbed—drive, sex, energy and self-care.

There may be no previous history of depression.

Some old people have strange delusions of bodily change. For instance, they fear that their bowels have become blocked so that they smell unpleasantly, that they have terrible diseases that could be transmitted, that their gums have rotted and, again, that this causes them to be unacceptable to others. Perhaps these delusions serve as an explanation for their isolation.

The apparent disturbance in brain function is not a true disability. The person may seem to have a poor memory, limited concentration and possibly some loss of acquired knowledge. Apathy is the main reason for this impression; the person has no real loss. All the other manifestations of apathy are present too. There is no interest in things that were previously important, self-care is neglected, social contacts are avoided, energy gives way to constant sleeping or sitting gazing into space and the sex drive is also lost. When a person ceases to care for him- or herself a dilapidation will be observed. If a person looks wild, unkempt, dirty and undernourished, the person looks similar to those suffering from a dementia and it is easy to assume that mental deterioration is the cause. Because of this, it is important to recall the lack of interest in the self that many of us experience under physical or emotional stress.

Symptoms can also imitate hypochondria—the person seems to be preoccupied with health problems and, even when there is a real physical problem, the symptoms are exaggerated. Panic reactions can occur. The person will breathe too frequently or heavily, have dizzy spells, palpitations and tremors and will be afraid that a heart attack or even death is imminent. Sleep patterns are disrupted, the person awakens very early in the morning and interest in food is lost. All these symptoms may be entirely new, but a history of depression is of significance.

It is important to be aware that if a person is suffering from a depression it is possible to persuade him or her into providing a perfectly good history. This may require a considerable amount of encouragement and patience, but if a clear, reasonable history is provided, it is highly unlikely that the person has a dementia-related disorder.

A careful, unstressful, yet encouraging discussion with patients will clarify the situation in most instances. Proper nourishment, good support and improved social outlets will result in a very different picture within a few days. Careful enquiry into possible problems at home or the existence of 'unsurmountable' difficulties such as bills mounting up, a cold house, a threatening neighbour or relative, can bring relief. With the assistance and guidance of social workers and others, the patients will begin to see that there are solutions. If there is something to live for, something to do, someone who cares and some solutions to worrying problems, people will start to respond more positively to living.

Appropriate medical treatment is indicated with depression as with any of the disorders associated with delirium. Some causes of depression are:

Physical illness

Drugs
Life review—reproach, guilt, self-criticism
Boredom
Bereavement
Loss of control
Loss in general
Previous personality which was prone to depression

Old people often forget which medicines to take, what the dose should be, and when and how often it should be taken. They forget when, or if, they took them at a previous time and even get mixed up over which medicine is the current one. Bathroom cabinets contain pills prescribed years before which may be totally inappropriate, and even dangerous. This all too frequently ends up with a drug cocktail and serious consequences.

When there is no one to talk to, nothing to read and little to do other than sit and think, life reviews are certain to take place. We all enjoy reminiscing, but few of us really like to think about bad times and failures. It is the good memory that pleases and is discussed. When loneliness leaves nothing but the past to consider, it is inevitable that the more depressing and unsatisfactory memories will surface. Self-reproach over the simplest errors of judgement can magnify the errors into unfor-giveable 'sins'. Ruminations can become night-mares that persist into daytime and assume such proportions that the person feels that his or her life-style has been wicked or criminal. This kind of negative reminiscence needs the support and guidance of a therapist or counsellor. Usually the self-reproach can be dispelled by kind and happy surroundings with caring people where the person can, once again, feel of some worth.

Boredom is something few of us can tolerate. Being sensorily or socially deprived is a form of brainwashing, yet it frequently happens to the sick and handicapped. Many old people are not sick or infirm, but are isolated due to lack of support from family or friends or insufficient finances, so a situation can quickly develop which allows a depression to take hold.

The experience of loss in a variety of forms is part of growing old. Status, finances, family, friends and social contacts are all vulnerable. We regard it as a right to be able to control our lives and what happens to us and even to control who we allow into our private world. Rarely is life that simple for the elderly. Not only is control of events and circumstances in jeopardy, but the ability to continue earning, taking action and gaining the respect of others are all subject to change.

Bereavement and the various possible illnesses preceding it are real threats to independence and peace of mind. Too frequently it becomes necessary to call on others for help instead of having the ability to make a self-assertive stand. There are thousands of older people who maintain their individuality until they die—often still actively pursuing their own concerns. However, there is also a large proportion of this older population who become isolated and vulnerable.

WHAT TO DO ABOUT DEPRESSION

Check on the presence of any of the signs listed above. Look for possible causes.

Take a careful history. Apart from clarifying many issues already mentioned clues might arise as to the most useful way to help the person.

Are relatives or friends exerting undue pressure? Is there some misunderstanding at home? There may be worry about bills or heating. Consider all aspects of the person's day-to-day living.

Alternatively, the unfortunate person may be being swamped by the number and variety of would-be helpers. Such over-protectiveness could stifle motivation and incentive.

Day Centres and key worker systems can minimise the many confusions, conflicting pressures and interference with daily living skills.

Common sense plays a major role in such situations and solutions may prove easier than first imagined.

A proper medical examination is important and the appropriate physician should be consulted. Where necessary the right medication can improve matters considerably.

Exercises

- ■Role-play the differences between confusion, delirium and depression.
- ■Provide a useful programme for care services from the community to an elderly depressed person which will preserve his/her independence and safeguard self-esteem.
- ■Role-play a situation which might provoke a depression in an elderly relative.

4

Odd Behaviour

From the dawn of time people have had problems in finding an explanation for matters beyond their knowledge or experience. In their reluctance to admit to ignorance they have managed to find ways in which to fill the vacuum. Most mythology or widely accepted 'fact' can be traced to some untested and unfounded theory offered by an ancient 'expert' or 'sage' which has been accepted without question by his or her adherents. The ageing process was and is a prime target. For instance, over the centuries witches have been depicted as old crones with tall pointed hats, yet newspapers and television accounts of witchcraft portray a much younger coven membership, clearly contradicting traditional beliefs. When closely examined most of the expectations and beliefs regarding age are not based on fact.

In every community there is the 'odd' character. Social gatherings are often the situation in which unacceptable behaviour is highlighted. Social mistakes irritate others, unusual responses are rarely forgotten. If the person is a recognised 'character' or local eccentric, then the behaviour is forgiven, even expected. Equally, someone seen as a 'delinquent' can rarely do anything right. However, if behaviour is unexpected and observers cannot account for it, the chances are that such behaviour

will provoke pejorative or highly critical remarks. The fact that a genuine reason for such reactions might be available—illness, head injury etc.—is overlooked. In hospital and residential homes, as well as in the community, there are many examples of behaviour which are outside normal experience and which are seriously misunderstood.

If a person neglects to go to the toilet and has an 'accident' in an inappropriate part of the ward or home the label 'incontinent' is soon attached to the notes. The circumstances surrounding this accident are not examined, common sense is overlooked and a proper enquiry is not made. Some possible reasons for this 'incontinence' include:

It is impossible to identify where the toilet is.

All the doors look the same.

There is a physical reason for urgency.

The person is unable to walk and requests for help have been ignored.

The person had a bad dream.

The person was intoxicated or drugs were causing problems.

Admittedly the person could be incontinent, or there could be another reason. There are innumerable physical and neurological causes.

Whatever form the 'odd' behaviour may take, jumping to conclusions is not going to provide the right answer with certainty. There are always alternative explanations and if misunderstanding is to be minimised it is important to consider the alternatives and ways to investigate which one could be correct.

Take, for example, a woman who is always walking into things. There are a number of possible explanations for this behaviour: she is blind; she does not concentrate on what she is doing; she is apathetic; clumsy; forgetful; she is 'miles away'. Another possibility is that a stroke or tumour could be causing her to neglect or ignore one side of her body, so she walks into those things which, to her, do not exist. Simple investigations include:

Eye tests.

Relevant tests and observations of memory, concentration and interest.

Does she respond to people standing to one side of her?

Does she leave food untouched on one side of the plate?

Does she start to read only from one part of the page and ignore the rest?

Does she hear things from only one side?

Does she try to dress only one side of her body?

Does she claim that one of her hands is not her own?

Those who, as a result of specific brain damage, neglect or ignore one side of their bodies, even to the extent of not hearing, seeing or responding to any stimulus from that side, are the subject of much misunderstanding. Being unaware of this anosognosia, as it is called, relatives and staff may misinterpret behaviour. For instance, a person may be called 'over-sexed' because he or she climbed into someone else's bed. If, after the patient returns from the toilet, the correct bed is in the area that is, to the person, non-existent, it is reasonable that he or she should get into a bed which is directly opposite and in the world he or she perceives.

It is not uncommon in hospital to find patients who will not get dressed without considerable fuss and assistance. Observers' explanations include: The person is unmotivated; lazy; attention-seeking; 'thinks we are servants' or 'goes into a daydream'. Other explanations could be:

The person may have a specific deficit in brain functions.

The person may not be able to differentiate the clothes from the object on which they are laid.

There could be a problem associating those clothes with the body and there is a feeling of helplessness as to what to do.

Tumours, strokes, impairments due to Alzheimer's disease etc. could be the cause.

How best to help depends on the person's needs. It is wise to try several approaches until a useful solution is found. Placing the clothes in order, miming what to do, physically helping them to get started or talking through each stage can all be helpful. The major aids are patience, understanding and encouragement.

A person can sing every word of a well-known song and yet will not converse properly with anyone. This is a common problem and gives rise to much misunderstanding. Observers believe that the person can talk but is being lazy, seeking attention or is just being difficult. But the real reason may be due to a variety of language deficits.

Language is usually the concern of the left hemisphere of the brain, in particular the temporal lobe. Rhythm, music and melody are the concern of areas in the right hemisphere. This is common to right-handed people. With left-handed people, the locations are often the same, but with a strong history of family left-handedness, or laterality, the dominance might be reversed, or there may be a mixed dominance—both hemispheres playing a role. In right-handed people then, if there is damage to the language centres, they may be problems with speech, reading and writing, but as rhythm, music and melody are in another system, these will continue to function normally. So a person may have problems in speaking properly but will possibly be able to sing a well-known song.

Before introducing a rehabilitation programme it is important to establish that language is

impaired. A proper assessment is necessary. Test to
see if the person can read or write, ask for the help of
a speech therapist to ascertain the level of retained
ability and then see if melody or rhythm can be used
to encourage some return of speech. For example,
can the person sing some simple words to the beat
of a rhythm—'cup of tea' or 'it's a nice day'—in
singing tones rather than spoken ones.

These are only a few examples of how behaviour
due to impairments of brain function can be
misinterpreted. Lack of awareness of these
possibilities can lead to added pressure and
unhappiness for the client.

Exercises

■Consult books and articles to collect definitions of
apraxia, aphasia, agnosia, agraphia and acalculia.
With these definitions consider behaviours that
you have observed from clients.

■Consider if these explanations could apply.

■Have you ever been misunderstood? Or have you
misunderstood others?

■Role-play a specific behaviour observed in a client
and seek the group's opinion on the implications
of such behaviour.

■Consider ways in which behavioural investigations could be provided.

■What contacts have you with disciplines such as
occupational therapy, speech therapy, physio-
therapy or clinical psychology? In what way
could such disciplines be of help to you and your
clients?

5
What is Dementia?

Discussion Topics

■What does dementia mean to you? What do you expect to see?

■What do you think causes dementia; is it a disease in its own right?

■What does the word mean to the general public?

The word was first used by Aretaeus, Physician of Cappodoccia, in AD 150. He was referring to the loss of thought processes in the aged, and was undoubtedly having problems in distinguishing between confusion, delirium and other conditions in the same manner as those following him throughout the centuries! No two books, no two writers, no two disciplines seem to be capable of providing a common definition. The use of the word has become so complicated and confounded that only a very few will attempt an explanation or offer a suggestion as to its possible meaning. At present, by far the most common use is to include it under a heading of 'organic brain syndromes' but this does not define it.

The problem will be examined in the following chapters in a logical order. We will look at the various definitions that have been offered and consider the effects that these definitions have had

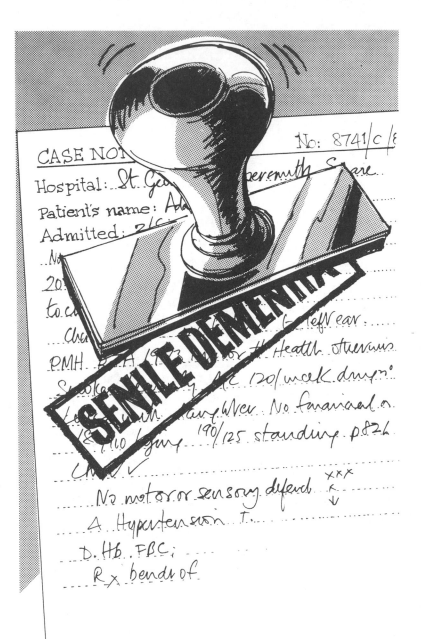

on staff working with the elderly and on the community in general. *Chapter 11* will attempt to gather together all the more recent findings with the intention of reaching a useful working definition.

To the general public dementia is often seen as a way to describe behaviour regarded as 'mad'. 'He is behaving in a demented manner' implies that the person is screaming, dancing about wildly and using crazy talk.

To professional staff, demented behaviour occurs when a person is unable to care for him- or herself, when social skills are lost and when forgetfulness and confusion are so marked that ridiculous errors are made. Cake ingredients are omitted, the gas is left on unlit, day and night are mixed up, milk is poured into the kettle and tea into the sugar bowl, and so forth. Disordered behaviour is accepted as one form of dementia—even as a definition. The dictionary does not help. Demented is defined as 'insane or crazy', and dementia is defined as 'insanity marked by complete mental deterioration'.

To many writers and professionals dementia is a disease in its own right. Senile dementia is used as a diagnosis, and particularly important is the differentiation between senile and pre-senile dementia. The logic of using such a diagnosis in the light of the many different disease processes involved appears to be irrelevant to the diagnostician.

Various definitions or operational approaches include:

An untreatable degenerative disorder of the central nervous system associated with mental and social deterioration.

A progressive, irreversible disorder associated with intellectual and social deterioration.

Persistent confusion, a senile or pre-senile state of deterioriation.

Brain failure can be intrinsic or extrinsic. Extrinsic failure includes delirium, and the acute confusional states. The function of the *whole* brain is impaired by disease originating from outside the brain. Intrinsic failure means that the function of the *whole* brain is impaired by diffuse structural disease which can have vascular or non-vascular causes.

Neuropathologists regard dementia as a disorder of neuronal metabolism that can show histological changes at biopsy or autopsy. They also look for histological evidence of the presence of certain cells. Neurologists refer to a symptom or syndrome characterised primarily by social and intellectual deterioration. They pose the question 'So, what is wrong?' and proceed to search for a variety of possible causes—tumours, head injuries, infections, strokes etc.

The World Health Organisation (1986) use the Royal College of Physicians', (London) (1982) definition of dementia as ' . . . the global impairment of higher cortical functions including memory . . . day to day living . . . learned perceptuo-motor skills, correct use of social skills . . . control of emotional reactions in the absence of gross clouding of consciousness. The condition is often progressive, but not necessarily irreversible'.

The recent American Classification system summarised below provides a series of signs to distinguish dementia, rather than define it.

Essential features
Global cognitive impairment
The intellect has been mature

Depression and acute confusional states are ruled out

Other signs
Intellectual, social and occupational dysfunction
Memory impairment
A related organic cause
Consciousness not clouded

Presence of one or more of the following:
Impaired judgement
Impaired thinking
Aphasia
Apraxia
Agnosia
Personality change

All of these offerings are open to criticism. As there are so many variations, the definitions add to the confusion and provide little guidance to staff in ascertaining what *is* wrong.

How can a person who functions quite well in many ways have 'global damage'? What, if any, is the difference between 'impairment' and 'damage'? In what way do all these lists of signs help to show the difference between global impairment and depression? If dementia is a disease in its own right, how can there be so many different signs?

This lack of continuity in meaning and interpretation, this lack of clarity, have resulted in staff, relatives and administrators accepting senile dementia as a diagnosis and also accepting the easiest to understand definition on offer. So 'senile dementia' and 'irreversible and progressive' have been adopted by all professions and the logic of the concept has been shelved.

The result of this over-simplification and these assumptions, is the belief that once this diagnosis has been reached there is nothing more to be done.

Continuing care is seen as the only solution and relatives as well as staff must take responsibility for the total management of the person so described. They are expected to provide a programme geared to total dependency while vaguely taking into consideration the staff's need for ease of management and relief from undue stress.

Questions have arisen about the assumption that the condition is irreversible since care staff have found that positive approaches such as reality orientation, reminiscence, environmental modification and normalisation have produced changes in many clients labelled as 'senile dements'. How can those who are suffering from an irreversible, progressive disease actually improve? Even more puzzling is the discovery that many clients so labelled do not have global impairments or damage. Some functions have been shown to be perfectly normal and in many cases very efficient.

Relatives are often bewildered by the variety of conflicting information presented to them. The media, as well as the professionals, talk about senile dementia and its progressive nature, and yet stroke clubs, the Alzheimer's Society, and other support groups all seem to suggest that there is something that can be done.

From everyone's point of view—professional staff, carers, relatives and the public—there is a need to tackle the question 'What *is* it?' and provide clear information and guidance on a subject which is continually being side-stepped. The relevant information *is* available, but because it is rather complicated and constantly changing as new findings are reported, there is a reluctance to put it together in a straightforward way.

Discussion Topics

■With such a variety of definitions to choose from, what would help you to understand the meaning of 'dementia'? Do any of the definitions help you?

■Look closely at the definitions in small groups. Discuss your response to them and compare different groups' opinions.

■What would *you* want to know that would really help in your work?

■Collect definitions from different books. See if there is a common theme. How do you think a workable definition could be found?

6

The Spiral or Danger Period

Discussion Topics

■ Have you ever been ill for at least two weeks? How did you feel as the acute stage of illness passed?

■ What sort of reactions have you noticed amongst those involved in a tragedy or traumatic event?

■ How would you react to a situation over which you had no control?

■ What emotional effects would imprisonment, internment or any form of enforced isolation have on you?

Most elderly people are reasonably healthy, independent, active and in charge of their own lives and environment. There are regular features and stories by the media about people who do remarkable things on their 100th birthday. Old people are many in number, but it is only the very remarkable ones who make the news. The 81-year-old who went sky-diving for the first time; the people in their 80s who take part in marathons, the postmistress who gave up work at 99 and celebrated her 100th birthday on Concorde; the vicar who, after preaching at his 100th birthday service, was delighted to accept some whisky as a present. All these people are worthy of news headlines.

However, there are many who also live to a great age quite quietly in their own way without making any notable contributions to the press. Thousands of people age normally, have normal problems and live in a normal manner, so everyone forgets that they exist.

If all things are equal, if health, finances, social support and outside interests are maintained, there is no reason for things to go wrong. However, a combination of traumatic events, personality factors and outside interference can have profound effects on an elderly person's well-being. If problems such as bereavement, medical complaints, physical traumas, or financial crises arise then a vicious circle may be set up very quickly.

The sick may become isolated, as can the bereaved. Self-care becomes increasingly unimportant. When finances are limited, fear of spending money begins to grow. Lack of self-care, lack of money for food, clothing and heating can lead to frailty, which in turn leads to illness followed by isolation and an increase in the problems. Not all old people have problems; much depends on their personalities and the support they have. Nevertheless, any onslaught on independence will weaken them to some degree. If the first vicious circle is created then it is not long before a spiral is in operation. This can lead to withdrawal and apathy, both of which lead to depression. Each of these factors can be compounded so that the person progresses to dilapidated appearance, a dilapidated physique and becomes mentally dilapidated too.

Although many are strong enough or resilient enough to cope on their own or have loving, supportive families to help, there are a large number of people who are vulnerable for a variety of reasons. Once their partner has died, for example, the person could be alone in the world. Physical illness or disability may be profound and financial loss may drastically change the person's life-style. The person may always have been of a dependent nature. All of these could increase personal vulnerability.

Once depression or apathy are well established, the spiral extends again. Stronger personalities may attempt suicide, but usually it is outside forces that play a major role at this stage. Hospitalisation or institutionalisation can be enforced and the relentless label of 'senile dementia' may be applied.

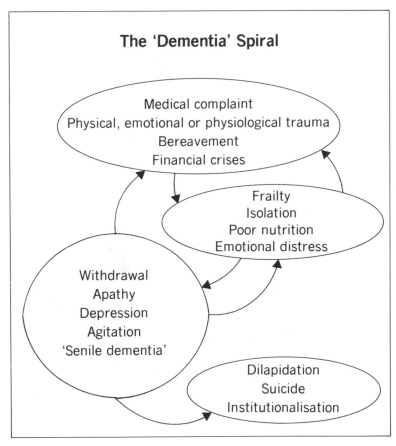

The 'Dementia' Spiral

Medical complaint
Physical, emotional or physiological trauma
Bereavement
Financial crises

Frailty
Isolation
Poor nutrition
Emotional distress

Withdrawal
Apathy
Depression
Agitation
'Senile dementia'

Dilapidation
Suicide
Institutionalisation

Unless disease processes have been in operation for some time previous to the trauma, the state described here is really a pseudo-dementia brought about by shock, worry or depression. Unless it is properly investigated and suitable approaches initiated, the person may well spend the rest of his or her life in a dependent state.

Exercises

■How should bereavement be handled? What can be done for an elderly person alone?

■What is the possibility of suicide amongst the elderly?

■What group is most liable to attempt suicide?

■What can the community do? What help is available to the lonely elderly? Find examples of possible pseudo-dementias in case notes and discuss probable explanations.

■List ways to help, or how to find help in the community near you

■Role-play different kinds of stress. Discuss ways to identify needs.

7

Reversible Dementias

Until recent years, thorough investigations of the brain using laboratory techniques held considerable dangers for the elderly patient. This is possibly one of the reasons for a continued belief in irreversible conditions. However, present techniques are no longer invasive or dangerous and have progressed so far that reversible conditions have been identified and defined. Illnesses once regarded as progressive, destructive and irreversible, have been isolated and methods have been developed to successfully restore a person to normal functioning and living.

Many eminent researchers and clinicians can now list potentially treatable disorders in which dementia has been featured. Among the states already identified by the researchers are the following:

Intracranial Conditions

Various forms of Obstructive Hydrocephalus

Normal Pressure or Communicating Hydrocephalus (NPH)

Subdural Haematomas

Intracranial Tumours.

Normal Pressure or Communicating Hydrocephalus is one of the more recent states for which treatment is possible. It can suddenly appear, usually between the ages of 50 and 65 years, and used to result in long-term care. It starts abruptly after some internal or external trauma to the brain. Three factors are present to indicate the possible diagnosis—a deterioration of intellectual ability, feet which are either 'glued' to the floor or are wide-based in walking, (this is ataxia) and incontinence, often double. Many of these patients respond to an operation (shunt) which drains off excess fluid and allows the person to return to normal living.

Metabolic or Nutritional Deficiencies
If the supply of nutrients is limited or there is some interference, intellectual impairments, or a dementia, will result. Some of the conditions include:

Anoxia (impaired oxygen supply to tissues) due to cardiac or pulmonary failure

Endocrine disturbances

Hypothyroidism

Vitamin deficiencies of many kinds, eg. B12, folate, thiamine etc.

Collagen diseases

Central nervous system infections, eg. neuro-syphilis, Wernicke's encephalopathy, meningitis etc.

Interventions appropriate to the particular disorder are frequently successful in reversing the mental deterioration or at least improving it.

Toxic Dementias
The side-effects of living in today's world can produce a dementia-related state. Poisons, toxins and viruses can all affect intellectual and social competence. In industry, chemicals, unless carefully managed, produce undesirable effects on the human brain. Problems can be relieved if the person is removed from contact with the dangerous

substance or environment, or is suitably protected. Long-term contact may well produce more severe damage or even prove fatal. Fortunately, industry is aware of the dangers and precautions are taken. Even so accidents do happen, people can be over-confident or careless. In agriculture there are further examples of poisons, noxious sprays and insecticides. Once again precautions are necessary, but faulty methods or equipment can cause accidents.

Overdoses of drugs, by accident or by design, glue-sniffing or excesses of alcohol are further dangers to brain function. The elderly are as prone to some of these 'accidents' as anyone else. The main source of problems is probably the medicine cabinet with its array of bottles collected over the years, all making it difficult for the old person to remember which one to take.

Alcohol, when taken in excess, can lead to Korsakow's psychosis as well as a variety of other problems. Alcohol abuse has long been regarded as an eventual cause of brain and other physical damage. Recent findings show that under certain conditions these effects can also be reversed.

Metal poisoning, eg. lead, is also a well recognised source of damage to brain function. This can now be treated.

In addition to conditions which have only recently become treatable, some well established signs of dementia are also under question. Brain size and weight used to be used as an indicator of whether or not a person had deteriorated, and it was assumed that shrinkage occurred with dementia. It has been shown that there is a great variability amongst individuals and so size and weight are not reliable forms of information. Enlarged ventricles found on brain scans were also thought to be diagnostic indicators. In view of the findings showing that enlarged ventricles may have no effect whatsoever on a person's level of functioning this 'sign' is also suspect.

There is a stream of information on new ways to identify illness, treatment and relevant indications of a real deterioration, so it is highly probable that yet more conditions will become reversible with treatment. This makes it even more imperative that each individual case should be examined with care.

Discussion Topics

■ Have you ever suffered from toxic effects due to gases, poisons etc?

■ In what way does the knowledge that a reversible condition might be the cause of your client's problem change your way of working?

■ What have you been told, in training or otherwise, about dementia?

■ Define senile dementia.

8
'Hardening of the Arteries'

Discussion Topics
■ Have you heard the expression 'hardening of the arteries'? What does it mean to you?
■ Is this what senile dementia really is?

Most people believe that real senility means that as you get older the arteries go hard and stiff so that the blood cannot circulate properly and so the blood supply to the brain gets cut off. Many professional staff also believe that vascular disturbance or arteriosclerosis in the brain is the main cause of a dementia process. Another belief states that if it is not caused by a vascular disorder then the problem is due to cell death. This appears to be related to a popular myth which holds that 100,000 cells die in the brain every day from the age of 21 years. In fact there is comparatively little cell loss in the normal brain.

It is now recognised that, despite the problems of arterial changes that might occur, only about 10 per cent of all states in which dementia is found is due to vascular causes. If no blood gets to the brain then death must follow; total blockage obviously implies death. Massive blockages are rare and are caused by malignant hypertension. The true role of vascular disease in dementia-related states remains unclear, and we must await the results of intensive research before its importance can be put into perspective. Undoubtedly the many different locations of a stroke can produce quite different symptoms, signs and malfunctions. These need to be carefully considered when a rehabilitation programme is being planned.

In the elderly, a stroke is far too frequently interpreted as a sign of dementia. As in any other age group, a person aged more than 60 can recover from a stroke or can be left with impairments of function. Admittedly, their rate of recovery is not quite as good as among younger people, but that does not imply that it is poor. Nor does it imply that survivors are subject to a dementia. Because a person loses some functional ability, it does not mean that he or she is mentally deteriorating.

The major vascular condition with which dementia is associated is called Multi Infarct Dementia (MID). Sometimes this is thought to imply global damage, but this is not so. Brains with global damage are the property of the dead, or of zombies. Global impairment is more acceptable as a description, but still improbable. The brain is a highly intricate piece of machinery and impairment of *every* system very rare indeed. Neuropsychological investigations which test different functions and abilities will unearth specific areas of damage and other areas which are either well preserved or which would respond to retraining.

MID may accompany Alzheimer's Disease. Either may occur before or after the onset of the other. This complicates the situation and makes diagnosis very difficult.

MID is usually diagnosed when the following are present:

An apparently abrupt onset.

Stepwise changes. A period of acute disability and illness is followed by a period of stability, which varies from person to person, before another stroke occurs. This process may occur again and again.

Neurological signs and symptoms are clear-cut, eg. aphasia, apraxia etc.

A history of hypertension is common.

A history of previous strokes is also common.

The course is fluctuating in severity—some episodes will be more severe than others.

So though a person may be rather hypertensive he or she may be living a reasonably normal life when a cerebrovascular accident occurs. There may have been some transient ischaemic attacks (mini-strokes) unnoticed by patient or family on previous occasions, but this event seems to come unexpectantly. If the person recovers, the recovery is accepted by patient and relatives and normal life is pursued as far as possible. However, if over several months or even years a number of strokes occur, leaving some degree of damage on each occasion, it is hardly surprising if the degree of impairment and permanent damage builds up and assumes serious proportions. Each new stroke may attack one area or a totally different one. The amount of recovery on each occasion can vary, so some functions can be badly affected while others may be only slightly impaired or not involved at all. It is, therefore, logical to examine for retained abilities, to locate areas of minimal impairment which would respond well to rehabilitation and to identify functions which appear to be lost. Retained abilities can be used by staff to encourage the person to regain confidence and at least some degree of independence.

It is not important here to provide an account of

the different effects on function that are sustained as a result of vascular catastrophes in different areas of the brain. Such information can be obtained from the many textbooks on the subject. What *is* important is to stress that damage is rarely global. Even when there have been a large number of strokes in different areas of the brain there will still be other areas capable of responding to treatment and some which have been totally spared (even though these are at times hard to find). In such circumstances a neuropsychologist is of help. If it proves impossible to obtain the assistance of a neuropsychologist, it is possible to screen for specific difficulties and retained function. There are several simple screening procedures available, eg. The Magazine Method (Holden and Woods, 1982) which provides useful guidelines. To ignore such possibilities is to limit the opportunities for recovery (if only partial) for those with MID.

It is also worth noting that in the case of people from another culture or nation, certain customs and beliefs must be kept in mind. Some races believe that they have been sent a 'trial'; that these 'trials' must be accepted not only by the recipient, but also by the family. Rehabilitation can prove difficult under these circumstances and requires the support of people from the same community. Some races have specific uses for particular limbs and if a stroke has impaired the use of, say a hand, it is possible that the catastrophe will have wider implications than might be thought usual. For example, certain normal self-care may prove hard to sustain—eg. washing, toileting.

Exercises and Discussion Topics

Is a stroke in an older person more likely to lead to a dementia than in a younger person?

What can happen if MID occurs with an Alzheimer-type process?

Think of cases with vascular problems and list retained abilities you have observed.

Is a person with a speech or language problem totally impaired?

What differences have you noticed amongst individuals who have had a cerebro-vascular accident?

What do you know of racial customs which might have a bearing on response to a stroke or other illness?

Role-play different types of problem which may be seen with stroke or MID patients. See if other members of the group can pick out the differences.

9
Diseases Associated with Dementia

There are words and terms which seem so complex and alien to us that we turn away and make no attempt to understand them. The parts of a car are a good example. To many of us, things like alternators, distributors and pistons are vague things that exist somewhere under the bonnet of a vehicle. But as to what they do, look like or where they can be found—that is the business of the garage!

Although medical terminology can at times seem awe-inspiring or outside our experience or need for knowledge, it is often worth taking a second look. A term like Subacute Sclerosing Panencephalitis is enough to widen one's eyes in disbelief and requires some concentration in order to even read it. It is natural to dismiss it as yet another of the medical profession's attempts to keep things a mystery. On the other hand if it is called SSPE, as it usually is, it does not seem so complicated, but equally, it does not inspire interest. However, if we are to attempt to appreciate the diseases associated with dementia, or more correctly, the diseases in which dementia occurs, we need to make a special effort to extend our knowledge of these 'mysterious' disorders.

Age is not an essential for dementia to be present. Even the very young can be victims. SSPE, mentioned above, is a result of a measles virus continuing to live in the child's body after the attack until the teens. Admittedly, the state is very, very rare, but it concerns children, not the old. The physical and intellectual deterioration due to SSPE are severe and, despite intensive research, the disease remains resistant to treatment, though there are promising signs. Meningitis and other viruses can also attack the young and cause serious brain damage.

In the middle years, other complaints can be found. These can attack older age groups and may be far from common. They include:

Pick's disease; Viral encephalopathies and transmissible viruses; Hydrocephalus; Multiple Sclerosis; Sub-cortical disorders such as Parkinson's disease, Huntington's chorea, thalamic disorders, and Korsakow's psychosis; Drug overdoses and massive ECTs; Head injuries. Many of these are manageable, for others treatment procedures are being developed, and research is working hard on others.

It is important to appreciate that dementia is *not* a disease in its own right. It can be found in all age groups, appear in many different forms and is only one factor in a variety of diseases and conditions. There is an urgency in each case to identify the disease process responsible so that the current form of treatment or management can be initiated as soon as possible. There may not be a known treatment, but this does not imply that 'nothing can be done'.

Detailed accounts of these diseases or conditions are not relevant here. Those who are interested are directed to the reference list which will provide further information about 'other' illnesses associated with dementia. There are many voluntary organisations who often know more about these diseases than the staff caring for such patients. The Alzheimer's Society, Huntington's chorea associations, Head Start (head injury), stroke clubs, Parkinson's disease support groups etc. are making it their business to learn all they can. If the need to understand and to help is recognised by lay people, surely it should follow that professionals should, at least, make similar efforts?

Exercises

It may be advisable for the group to concentrate on one disorder at a time. Pictures, demonstrations, role playing or individual study of relevant, straightforward books (see below) would at this point be appropriate. Group discussion would follow from the reading.

The results of a request to a department of neurology for permission to attend a ward round or case conference concerning any relevant cases might prove rewarding.

Suggested Reading

Strub RL and Black FW, *Organic Brain Syndromes*, FA Davis Company, Philadelphia, 1981.

Mayeux R and Rosen WG (eds), 'The Dementias', Volume 38, *Advances In Neurology*, Raven Press, 1983.

Cummings JL and Benson DF, *Dementia: A Clinical Approach*, Butterworths, 1983.

Mann DMA and Yates PO, 'The Ageing Brain', *Geriatric Medicine*, pp. 275—81, April 1983.

Holden UP and Woods RT, *Reality Orientation*, Chapter 5, Churchill Livingstone, 1982.

10
Alzheimer's Disease

Discussion Topics
- What is the difference between Alzheimer's disease and senile dementia?
- What is the cause of Alzheimer's disease? Can you 'catch' it?
- What do you expect to see in a typical Alzheimer patient?

Before looking into details on this subject it is important to establish the level of knowledge of the group, and an individual's conception of the implications of commonly used terms.

In 1898 Alzheimer found that certain lesions in the brains of the elderly were nothing to do with arteriosclerosis. By 1907 Alzheimer reported finding senile plaques in the brain of a woman aged 51 years who was suffering from dementia. In 1910 Kraeplin, in his new classification of mental illnesses, gave the name Alzheimer's disease to those states in which dementia occurred before the age of 60 years, where senile plaques and neuro-fibrillary tangles could be identified.

It is only within recent years that the problem of how to distinguish a pre-senile state from a senile one has been closely examined. It is now accepted that the only difference is the second of time between 64 and 65 years for men and 59 and 60 years for women. 'Pre-senile' is nothing more than an expression of ageism as there is no distinct process which can be attributed to the under- or over-60s. There *is* a variation in the process when it develops after the age of 80 years, as it appears that the later in life that Alzheimer's disease manifests itself the less damage there is to the brain and to the personality. Conversely, the earlier it presents the greater the cell loss, growth of abnormal cells and loss of neurotransmitters.

Other variations are related to inherited or familial strains or to the damage caused in specific brain areas where the abnormal cells proliferate. These variations are still under investigation.

Approximately 1.5 million people in the USA and 50 per cent of all cases in Britain with a disorder involving a dementia suffer from Alzheimer's disease. Undoubtedly this is a major cause of mental deterioration. However, it does need to be seen in the context of the thousands of elderly people who remain fit and independent, or simply ill and frail.

What *is* Alzheimer's disease? What causes it, and how can it be differentiated from an ordinary confusion? These are the main questions concerning not only carers but also researchers. Alzheimer isolated the neurofibrillary tangles and senile plaques typically present. Granulo-vascular degeneration and Hirano Body formations are also found. What does this information mean to the average carer, relative or staff member with a basic training? The answer is not a lot—the terms are too complicated!

Most staff find it easier to assume that age and deterioriation go hand in hand. It is hard to accept the fact that many very old people are more intelligent than those that care for them. Equally, in view of expectations, it is difficult to come to terms with the idea that something *must* happen to the brain to cause loss of ability. Age alone does *not* imply loss of ability. Alzheimer's disease *is* a disease. Institutions encounter it every day. It is this disease that leads so many people to make unjustified generalisations regarding older people.

Research has identified areas to examine in order to test theories about the cause of Alzheimer's disease. Every week new findings are being added to the store of information on dementia and Alzheimer's disease. Let us look at some suggestions or hypotheses concerning the causes of this disease.

Inherited Abnormality

Studies suggest that about 20 per cent of relatives have developed Alzheimer's disease by the age of 80 years. There is a strong case for the existence of Familial Alzheimer's disease (FAD) and that there is a genetic factor responsible for this sub-type of the disease. Not all cases run in families, but there appears to be a strain which can be inherited.

Abnormal Structures

There is no doubt that neurofibrillary tangles, senile plaques and other abnormal cells are present in the brains of patients with Alzheimer's disease. Some of these are found in normal brains, but it is the numbers and their collection on specific sites in the brain which are associated with the disease process. The tangles are said to be more important in Alzheimer's disease and the more reliable indicator. Granulo-vascular degeneration of cells in the hippocampus is also found in increased numbers.

What causes these cells to grow remains unclear, but their presence is a diagnostic feature.

Research has provided evidence of brain plasticity, not only in the brains of children, but also in those ageing normally. Cells can and do regenerate and dendritic growth has been found. The implications of this regeneration remain as yet unclear, but it has been shown that such regeneration *does not* occur in the brains of Alzheimer's disease patients.

Infectious Agents

Could Alzheimer's disease be transmitted in some way? Viral diseases can be transmitted; why not Alzheimer's? Despite careful research, no evidence has been found to demonstrate this possibility. It does not appear to be infectious, though further enquiry is being made into this hypothesis.

Toxins

Could there be some noxious substance which could precipitate Alzheimer's disease? Lead, aluminium salts, zinc and other metals have been considered as possible influences or potential agents which could aid the development of abnormal cells. Tinned food has been examined as a possible source of the problem. Years of investigation are beginning to produce evidence to support the idea that toxins, or metals, have a role to play.

Neurotransmitters

Neurotransmitter malfunction plays a large part in the precipitation or development of certain disease processes. One of the most important findings in recent years is the fact that impairments in the production of certain of these neurotransmitters occur in Alzheimer's disease. One of the first systems to be implicated was the cholinergic one, where a deficiency in the enzyme Choline Acetyltransferase (CAT) was discovered. The activity of this enzyme correlates both with the degree of intellectual deficit and with the number of tangles and plaques present in the brain. Other neurotransmitters, eg. noradrenaline and dopamine, are also deficient when Alzheimer's disease is present. Work on the importance of neurotransmitters is extensive and is providing rewarding results.

It is important to note that normal ageing brains do not have the neurotransmitter or cell losses that are found in Alzheimer's disease. Cell loss occurs in damaged or diseased brains, whereas in normal brains there is comparatively little loss. This is one of the arguments contradicting the myth which implies that age and deterioration are synonymous. Alzheimer's disease is not an accelerated ageing process.

What parts of the brain could be affected?

The temporal lobe appears to be the most vulnerable. Behavioural changes associated with this area occur in the majority of Alzheimer's disease patients. Language disorders, apraxias, placing objects in the mouth, constantly feeling things and memory problems are all related in some way to temporal lobe disturbances. Furthermore, atrophy of this lobe is more common with Alzheimer's disease, as are concentrations of abnormal cells in this area, than in other parts of the brain. The cholinergic system is more impaired here too.

The parietal lobe is also affected. Constructional apraxia—difficulty in finding the way, in putting things together or in doing something like knitting are all frequently found, and these activities are all under the control of parietal lobe function.

Stages in the development of Alzheimer's disease

Stage 1

The subtle signs at this stage are often overlooked. Emotional responses *may* be the first to be affected. Feelings of apathy are common. People may complain of groundless illnesses, or deny that there is anything wrong. Depression or anxiety may be present. Restlessness, fatigue, and lack of initiative can alternate. Memory impairment is by far the most obvious sign. Recent memory is most particularly effected, long-term memory is barely touched. New situations or experiences cause problems. If a new problem-solving situation arises the patient quickly gets into difficulties. Routine or well-learned tasks are not affected.

Comprehension may not be so sharp. Often there is a hesitation in comprehension or the expression of ideas. Abstract thinking, judgement and understanding of maps, for instance, can be noticeably impaired in comparison to normal, previous responses. The woman who has been knitting for years has difficulty with a pattern, the cook cannot follow a new recipe, the mechanic cannot put a machine back together. In the early stages there are occasional examples of this difficulty. As time goes on these difficulties occur more frequently and become more noticeable. At this point there are no neurological signs to aid diagnosis.

Stage 2

This may be reached fairly quickly, or a year or two might lapse before some of the signs outlined above occur more frequently or become more profound. Normal living or working becomes increasingly difficult to sustain. Language is particularly affected. Word-finding difficulties (anomia) are common, there is difficulty in keeping to a topic, the conversation can go around in circles or off at tangents. Perseveration (the repetition of words, phrases or actions) might have begun. Wandering, restlessness and night disturbance can occur. Those with insight become more depressed and anxious and may well appear more deteriorated than they really are.

Stage 3

Apraxias, aphasias and agnosias will be more pronounced. Comprehension is affected. Personality, which up to this point has been intact, is now beginning to change. Emotional outbursts unrelated to circumstances may occur. Neurological signs are much clearer and more common. Incontinence, unusual reflexes, picking actions and possibly odd mouthings appear at this point. Reality has little meaning, even familiar faces become unrecognised.

Final Stage

Withdrawal and apathy intermingled with emotional outbursts, muttering, perseveration and even a fixed and vacant look belong to the very late stages of Alzheimer's disease.

The life span for a sufferer is seven years on average, but some patients could live for twenty years, while others may only survive for a few months. In black and white, the Alzheimer's disease story is a bleak one. Fortunately, real life is in Technicolor, and while it is important to know about the seriousness of the problem, the usual course of the disease and the research, it is equally important to appreciate that such knowledge can help to fight the process and provide guidelines for retraining or management.

Not all patients lose all ability. Efforts can be made to help them to maintain a good level of functioning, to cope with the anxiety, and to use their retained abilities effectively. Dependency will be reinforced if they are denied opportunities to care for themselves. Over-protectiveness can only lead to further losses, more apathy and withdrawal. It is of vital importance to provide appropriate assessment, to investigate closely the individual's routines, habits, interests, skills and history. It is also vital to recognise the necessity of providing the psychological framework that is needed by every human being—dignity, self-respect, choice, realistic independence, a group identity or membership (or at least some reasonable relationship with others) and sufficient stimulation to encourage engagement with things and interests as well as people. The environment should allow for privacy, self-care, and should be stimulating and home-like. With such a positive atmosphere total dependence and the inhumanity of wards and homes filled with babbling, withdrawn and dilapidated old folk awaiting death without dignity are minimised.

Exercises and Discussion Topics

■ How helpful is it to you to know more about the various disorders with which dementia is associated? Does it make a difference to the way you work?

■ How important is it to staff and carers, and relatives, to know that 'something can be done'?

■ Do you think you, your unit, other staff, should keep up-to-date on research? How could this be done?

■ What are you doing to encourage independence and the use of retained abilities?

■Invite relatives to explain what it is like living with a relative with Alzheimer's disease.

■Ask relatives what was the most difficult thing to cope with at home. Find out what relatives really needed to cope at home.

■Discuss in groups what your unit has been able to do which has shown changes in your patients with Alzheimer's disease.

■Collect recent articles on Alzheimer's disease and set up a seminar to discuss them.

11

Towards a
Definition of Dementia

Until recently the belief that dementia was a disease in its own right remained unchallenged. Probably, even now, few workers think of it as anything else. It is said to be a progressive, irreversible state about which little can be done. In the light of the number of disorders involved and the variety of causes it is no longer logical to encourage this belief.

This 'definition' is yet another example of loose thinking about the ageing process where age and loss of abilities are regarded as synonymous. Training programmes frequently avoid looking at the subject of dementia in depth and staff are left to interpret for themselves the meaning and implications of a label saying 'senile dementia'. Sometimes, because writers and researchers have failed to clarify the issue, the training staff have insufficient information too.

Over the age of 60 years *any* confusion can be labelled 'senile dementia'. This will guarantee that the majority of people will assume that the person is incapable of any self-care, skill or ability. If this is what they have been led to believe it is not surprising that so many patients receive inappropriate, or even harmful, 'care'.

To minimise error, misunderstanding or misinterpretation, not to mention wrong diagnoses, it is vital to look closely at each individual case. Thorough investigation is essential:

Confusion of a transient or physical nature must be identified.

Delirium and its causes must be treated.

If depression is the cause of an apparent dementia, then it is this which requires attention.

If these investigations fail to elicit an explanation then neurological and neuropsychological investigations should ensue.

Laboratory and technological investigations will assist in ascertaining the nature of the problem.

Treatable disorders of brain function should then be considered.

If the investigations point to a disorder with a dementia, the nature of this disorder should, as far as possible, be identified.

Each of the dementia syndromes has a particular pattern. This, in turn, indicates which treatment, retraining, rehabilitation or management programme is required or relevant. By doing this it is possible to provide optimal opportunity for the client to obtain appropriate help and a satisfactory quality of life.

The point here is that if a patient has a temperature it (the temperature) is not regarded as a disease, but as a symptom. This symptom is caused by a disease process. When the disease process is successfully treated the temperature returns to normal. A dementia is not present unless a disease process with which it is associated has afflicted the patient. If a dementia is not a disease itself, but is in fact caused by a disease or disorder, then it must be dependent on that disease or disorder. Therefore, as with a temperature, which is also dependent on its cause, if the disease responds to treatment so will the dementia.

During an illness a temperature can be lessened and the patient made more comfortable. It is also possible to control or influence a dementia in many ways. All the reversible states previously outlined respond in varying degrees to treatment; so does the dementia accompanying them.

Some disorders have, as yet, no known treatment (eg. Jacob-Creutzfeldt's disease) therefore the dementing process will progress alongside them. Other disorders can be controlled. Obviously here the dementia will also be controlled.

It is illogical, in view of this, to refer to dementia as an irreversible, progressive state. The course, development and reversibility of a dementia are, for the most part, dependent on the course, development and reversibility of the *disorder by which a dementia is caused.*

The term 'senile dementia' only refers to age and the fact that a dementing process is present. Once it was used to imply Alzheimer's disease in the over-60s. In practice it covered Alzheimer's and anything else with which a dementia was associated— providing the person was over 60 years of age. The term does not provide any information on cause, the disorder involved, possible treatment, the presence of retained ability, nor does it indicate what useful programme might be initiated. There is no distinct disorder called 'senile dementia'. Too often it is a term implying lack of interest in investigating further, or of providing carers with guidance on what to do next. Admittedly, with those patients in the late stages of an illness, or who are of an extreme age and frailty, a diagnosis is irrelevant. Only Tender Loving Care is of value. This does not justify the generalised use of a meaningless phrase or non-existent disorder.

Many scientists now refer to the Dementia Syndromes. A syndrome is a specific collection of certain signs and symptoms. This is more helpful than calling dementia a disease. It does imply that a number of disorders are involved and suggests that dementia takes different forms. It might be useful to regard dementia as a symptom of some disorder. However, it does vary from case to case and different functions and abilities can be effected with individuals afflicted by the same disorder. Alzheimer's disease and MID are the most common disorders associated with dementia found on wards and in homes. Each of these disorders has a different pattern, course and development and each requires a different care programme. Each case is different too, so an individual requires a specifically tailored programme to meet his or her needs.

Reasonable working definitions to use might be:

Confusion A state of clouded or disordered consciousness, usually of a transitory or temporary nature.

Dementia An impairment of intellectual and social functioning which is the result of a specific disease process.

At least this last definition would inspire the natural question 'What disease?' to be followed by 'What can be done?'

Exercises and Discussion Topics

- Role-play and/or list different disorders in which dementia occurs.
- Discuss clients that have been labelled 'senile dement'. Examine the reasons. Consider the retained functions.
- Look at written accounts or definitions of dementia. Discuss them.
- Try to find a useful, logical and meaningful definition of dementia that will prove helpful to all staff.
- Discuss the definitions of Confusion and Dementia outlined above.
- Canvas opinions as to the meaning of dementia among other staff, other disciplines, carers, relatives, the media and lay people.
- Read and discuss with the group:

Wilcock GK, 'Dementia' in *Recent Advances in Medicine*, AM Dawson, ND Compston, and GN Besser (eds) Churchill Livingstone (1984).

World Health Organisation, *Dementia in Later Life: Research and Action*, Technical Report Series, 730, Geneva (1986).

12

Conclusions

The present climate in gerontology—the study of ageing—is an exciting one. Research is putting mythology and general beliefs under the microscope and finding that most of them are based on false premises. Statistics are showing that the elderly are living longer. Instead of this being heralded as a break-through, it is regarded with apprehension, and there is concern about the growing number requiring long-term care—now tamely called 'continuing care'. It is true that there has been an increase in the numbers needing some care, but it must be remembered that there has also been a big increase in the numbers living to a healthy old age, pursuing life in their own independent way. Of the approximately 9 million people over 60 years of age in Great Britain, only 5 to 7 per cent have need of care owing to a deterioration process. 40 per cent of the over-85s do *not* need help and 50 per cent live at home and can get out. To overlook these facts is to ignore the active elderly and make ageing into a fearsome business. Furthermore, only 2 per cent of those between 60 and 70 years of age, and 20 per cent of those over 80 years of age are recorded as having a disease process which involves a dementia (Royal College of Physicians, 1982; Craig, 1983).

Recent surveys imply that the incidence of 'dementia' is declining. Although the results of these surveys still require wider confirmation, the signs are encouraging. The question that must be asked in view of this is, 'Why?' There are a number of possible explanations:

Better diagnoses. Modern investigations are less hazardous and more thorough. Physical illnesses are treated, delirium and non-dementia type confusions are investigated.

Knowledge of depression and its diagnosis and treatment is more widespread.

Reversible states and their treatment programmes are better understood and delineated.

More effort and interest is being given to the understanding of the ageing process by an ever growing number of disciplines.

More pressure is being exercised by organisations concerned with the well-being of the elderly.

Researchers are being encouraged and the well of knowledge is being filled.

The outmoded system of total care is being discouraged and positive approaches and programmes are being offered in hospitals, homes and in the community.

The individual needs, strengths, abilities and interests of the patient are becoming important in initial assessments prior to placements for treatment, retraining or rehabilitation programmes.

Normalisation now plays a prominent role— searching for ways in which individuals can pursue life according to their own personal taste, interests and routines.

Institutions are becoming more aware of their limitations in putting their concerns and policies before the needs of their clients.

As yet there is no miraculous cure for a large number of the disorders with which dementia is associated. Perhaps, in some cases, there never will be, but new methods to improve conditions and management are being introduced.

There is a conviction among many scientists that the next ten years will see vast improvements in knowledge, treatment and prevention. The pessimists are ignoring the facts already before them. Change *has* occurred in the last five to ten years. Reversible conditions have been isolated and many people, once potential candidates for a long-term ward, have been returned home to normal living. Others are sufficiently recovered to only require some help from the community. Hospitals and homes which once housed row upon row of living dead in miserable and humiliating surroundings are now, mostly, bright and more homely, encouraging self-care and control of the environment.

Outside the medical profession all the other disciplines—carers, relatives and voluntary organisations—are playing a major part in adapting institutions and homes into active, stimulating environments. They help in promoting self-care, the recognition of retained skills and encourage independence. All of which make life worth while, not just for the afflicted person, but also for the carers concerned.

The list of positive approaches grows ever longer. Conferences, courses, training programmes and scientific literature are available, but they need to be used or their value will be lost to potential clients.

Reality orientation; reminiscence; group living; music, drama, and exercise therapies; cognitive therapy; group and individual psychotherapies; family therapy and goal-setting guides etc. are all in current use and information on them is easy to obtain. Providing a service to elderly people without being aware of at least some of these approaches is akin to living in the Dark Ages. It is hoped that the blossoming private sector does not fail to take more than a look at this expanding field of knowledge and resource.

Unfortunately, the happier picture is not widespread. Much more is required to ensure that normalisation occurs in all institutions or care settings. Training and information for both staff and carers has been lacking and, despite improvements, is often outdated. There is recognition of the needs of *all* involved to possess relevant knowledge, but much depends on the ability and resources of the training departments.

There is still some resistance to acceptance of progressive or positive approaches. This is really in the hands of the policy makers, the trainers and the well-trained professionals to influence the climate for change. An informed media could do much for the older generation by keeping the public well informed about new ideas and approaches which take so long to filter through to the man in the street. If there was less confusion about confusion the growing elderly population would provoke less fear. If dementia was seen in perspective perhaps old age would not be so closely associated with it.

If the dread of ageing was relieved perhaps the process of ageing would become a more pleasant prospect and provoke optimistic instead of negative expectations.

Discussion Topics

■ Where are we going; what changes might research promote?
■ What contributions can *we* make to the treatment of those with a dementia?

■ Plan an ideal unit policy which would provide every opportunity for elderly people to function as normally as possible.

■ Role-play the right and wrong ways to discuss the future of a client with a dementia, both with that client and with his or her relatives.

Bibliography

Craig J, 'Growth of the Elderly Population', *Population Trends*, pp. 28–33, Summer 1983.

Cummings JL and Benson DF, *Dementia: A Clinical Approach*, Butterworths, (1983).

Hanley I and Gilhooly M, *Psychological Therapies for the Elderly*, Croom Helm, (1986).

Holden UP and Woods RT, *Reality Orientation: Psychological Approaches to the 'Confused' Elderly*, Churchill Livingstone, (1982).

Mann DMA and Yates PO, 'The Ageing Brain', *Geriatric Medicine*, pp. 275–81, April 1983.

Mayeux R and Rosen WG (eds), *The Dementias*, Vol 38, Advances in Neurology, Raven Press, (1983).

Royal College of Physicians, *Organic Mental Impairment in the Elderly*, Report of the Royal College of Physicians, London, (1982).

Strub RL and Black FW, *Organic Brain Syndromes*, Davis, Philadelphia, (1981).

Wilcock GK, 'Dementia' in *Recent Advances in Medicine*, Vol 19, Dawson AM, Compston ND and Besser GN (eds), Churchill Livingstone, (1984).

World Health Organisation, *Dementia in later life: Research and Action*, Technical Report Series, 730, Geneva, (1986).